Beyond Pluto

ELAINE LANDAU

Children's Press®
A Division of Scholastic Inc.
New York Toronto London Auckland Sydney
Mexico City New Delhi Hong Kong
Danbury, Connecticut

Content Consultant

Michelle Yehling

Astronomy Education Consultant

Aurora, Illinois

Reading Consultant

Cecilia Minden-Cupp, PhD

Early Literacy Consultant and Author

Library of Congress Cataloging-in-Publication Data

Landau, Elaine.
 Beyond Pluto / by Elaine Landau.
   p. cm.—(A true book)
 Includes bibliographical references and index.
  ISBN-13: 978-0-531-12565-6 (lib. bdg.)   978-0-531-14787-0 (pbk.)
  ISBN-10: 0-531-12565-3 (lib. bdg.)   0-531-14787-8 (pbk.)
 1. Pluto (Dwarf planet)—Juvenile literature. I. Title. II. Series.
 QB701.L35 2007
 523.48'2—dc22   2007012280

All rights reserved. Published in 2008 by Children's Press, an imprint of Scholastic Inc. Published simultaneously in Canada. Printed in the United States of America.
SCHOLASTIC, CHILDREN'S PRESS, A TRUE BOOK, and associated logos are trademarks and/or registered trademarks of Scholastic Inc.
1 2 3 4 5 6 7 8 9 10 R 17 16 15 14 13 12 11 10 09

Find the Truth!

Everything you are about to read is true *except* for one of the sentences on this page.

Which one is **TRUE**?

T or F The Kuiper Belt was discovered by an astronomer who couldn't see it.

T or F No spaceship has ever traveled beyond Pluto.

Find the answer in this book.

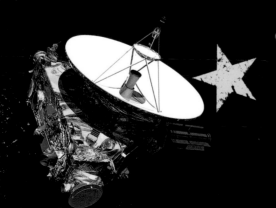

Contents

THE **BIG** TRUTH!

The Hubble
Space Telescope

The Hubble Space Telescope orbits above Earth's atmosphere.

There may be as many as 70,000 objects in orbit beyond Pluto.

Pluto is far away from the sun.

In North America, this group of stars is called the Big Dipper. In other parts of the world it has other names, such as the Plow and the Wagon.

CHAPTER 1

A Trip Beyond Pluto

We see the stars in the Big Dipper as they looked many decades ago.

When you look up at the sky on a starry night, do you wonder about what else is out there? Are there planets that have not yet been discovered? Could there be other forms of life? No one knows the answers to these questions. But **astronomers** are busy trying to find out!

Tiny organisms have existed on Earth for millions of years. One example is this protist, seen through a microscope. Scientists are looking for life forms such as this on other planets.

Someday it might be possible for astronauts to travel beyond Pluto. But for now, you will have to imagine what a trip would be like. To start, you would have to pack enough supplies to last at least 20 years. It takes about 10 years to reach beyond Pluto. But then you have another 10 years of travel before you're back to Earth!

These four planets are called gas giants because they are huge planets made mostly of liquid and gas.

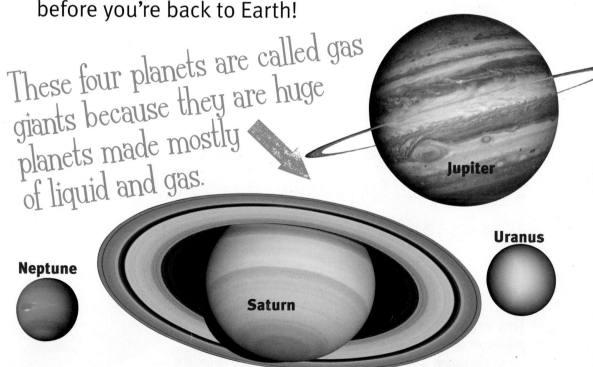

This illustration lets you compare the sizes of the four gas giants.

Your trip would begin by blasting off in a spaceship. Powerful rockets would push you through Earth's **atmosphere**. An atmosphere is a blanket of

This image was taken from a space shuttle in 1998. It shows the Mir space station above heavy clouds in Earth's atmosphere.

gases that surrounds a planet or a moon.

When you looked out the window of your spaceship, you would see a black sky and thousands of stars. You would see Earth get smaller and smaller as you moved farther away. You might see Mars, then perhaps giant Jupiter. About four years later, you might fly by Saturn with its beautiful rings. Finally, you would travel past Uranus and Neptune. You would then see one of the **dwarf planets** called Pluto.

Astronomers think the Kuiper Belt contains the remains of materials that formed the planets billions of years ago.

Pluto is in a region called the **Kuiper Belt** (KY-pur belt). It is several billion miles from the sun. From your spaceship, you would see thousands of rocky, icy objects flying through space. These objects are called Kuiper Belt Objects, or **KBOs**. Like the planets, KBOs **orbit**, or travel around, the sun.

Astronomers discovered the Kuiper Belt in 1992. What have they learned about this area and its strange objects? What else do we know about this region beyond Pluto? Let's find out.

The diameter of the largest known KBO is less than the distance across the United States.

This is an illustration of Eris (left), the largest known KBO, and its moon, Dysnomia (right).

11

This drawing shows the sun
lighting up Pluto. In reality, the
sun would look many times smaller
from Pluto than it does here.

sun

Pluto

CHAPTER 2

The Kuiper Belt

The first spacecraft sent to Pluto is expected to arrive in 2015.

Pluto used to be called a planet. Then astronomers started discovering KBOs. Pluto seemed more like these KBOs than a planet. For a while, astronomers thought Pluto was both a KBO and a planet. But that became confusing. One KBO was even bigger than Pluto. Should it be called a planet, too? What would you do if you were an astronomer?

A Man Ahead of His Time

Some astronomers "found" the objects at the edge of our **solar system** before they could see them. In 1951, American astronomer Gerard Kuiper suggested there was a ring of icy objects at the edge of our solar system. He said that these objects might be **comets**.

Kuiper used math and his knowledge about space to form his idea. However, no telescope was powerful enough to see to the edges of the solar system and to prove his idea.

By 1991, astronomers had more powerful telescopes. The next year, they saw Kuiper's ring of objects. It was named the Kuiper Belt in his honor.

What Is a Planet?

Is Pluto a KBO? Are some KBOs planets? Astronomers couldn't agree. Some wanted to add three more planets to the solar system. Others said no. Astronomers finally agreed on one thing. They needed to decide on the difference between a planet and other space objects.

Should Sedna and Quaoar (KWA-whar) be planets? They orbit the sun beyond Pluto.

Sedna
800-1100 miles in diameter

Quaoar
(800 miles)

Pluto
(1400 miles)

Moon
(2100 miles)

Earth
(8000 miles)

Members of the International Astronomical Union voted that Pluto does not fit the definition of a planet.

Some astronomers still think Pluto should be a planet — and there should be 12 planets in all.

Astronomers held a meeting in August 2006. Finally, they voted on the definition of a planet. They decided that a planet has to meet three conditions:

1 It has to be nearly round in shape.

2 It has to orbit a star, as Earth orbits the sun. This means the object can't be a moon.

3 It has to be big enough to have cleared out its orbit of other objects.

Pluto almost made it. It is round. It orbits the sun. But it has not cleared its orbit. That means it doesn't have enough **gravity** to pull on objects in its path and move them out of the way.

Based on these rules, Pluto could not be a planet anymore. Astronomers decided to call Pluto a dwarf planet.

There are lots of KBOs in Pluto's region of the solar system. Since 1992, more than 1,000 KBOs have been discovered. But we don't know much about them. These objects are billions of miles away. The sun's light is weak there. It is difficult to see them, even with the most powerful telescopes.

This Kuiper Belt Object is not round, so it could not be a planet.

The Solar System

Pluto (dwarf planet)

Uranus

Jupiter

Mars

Mercury

asteroid belt

Kuiper Belt Objects

- Number found so far: More than 1,000
- Largest: Eris (one-fifth the size of Earth)
- Farthest from sun: Sedna, about 82 billion mi. (132 billion km)

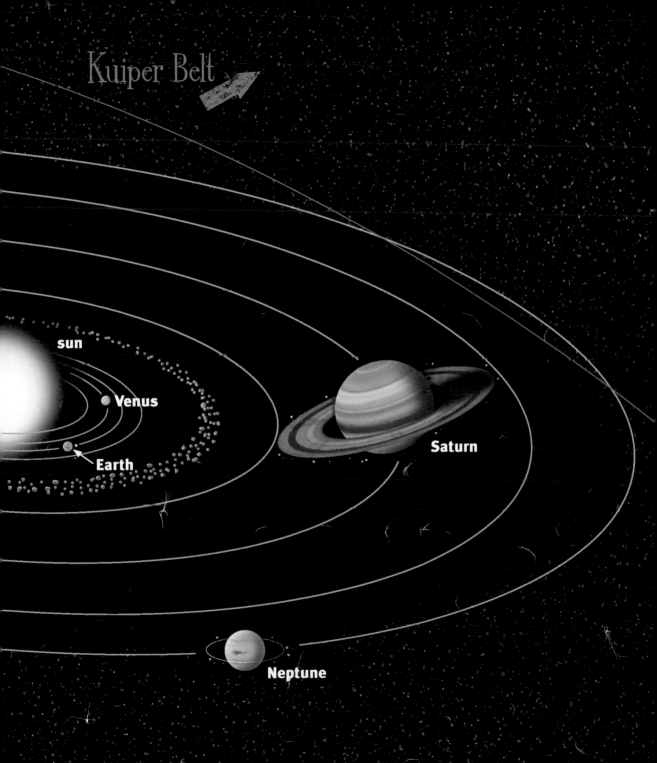

Kuiper Belt

sun

Venus

Earth

Saturn

Neptune

This artwork shows two KBOs.
The ringed planet is Neptune.

CHAPTER 3

What Do We Know About KBOs?

← Neptune's gravity pulls some KBOs right out of the Kuiper Belt.

If you traveled beyond Pluto, you would see that KBOs are made of rocks and ice. They range in size. Pluto is one of the larger KBOs. Others are perhaps only a few hundred miles across, or smaller.

Huge antennas such as this can receive radio signals from space probes a billion miles away.

21

Eris

The largest KBO was discovered in 2003. Its name
is Eris (AIR-is). Eris is even bigger than Pluto. Some
astronomers thought it would be the 10th planet.
It doesn't fit the new rules for identifying a planet,
however. Eris is now the largest known dwarf planet.

Astronomers think Eris, at its farthest point, is
about 9 billion miles (14 billion km) from the sun.
This is about three times farther from the sun than
Pluto. Pluto needs 248 Earth years to orbit the sun
once. But it takes Eris 560 Earth years to complete
a single orbit.

Some people wanted to
call Eris the 10th Planet.

Dysnomia

Eris

Telescopes cannot
see Eris as clearly as
it is drawn here. But the
Hubble Space Telescope
did measure its diameter.
Eris is 1,490 miles (2,400 km)
across. Eris's moon is
called Dysnomia
(dis-NOME-ee-ah).

Astronomers believe that Eris, like Pluto, is made of rock and ice. Eris is possibly whitish or light gray. Astronomers think that Eris's color comes from the ice that surrounds it. Eris is so cold that if it has an atmosphere, it might be frozen.

At some points in its orbit, Eris is closer to the sun than at other points. Scientists think that when Eris is closer to the sun, the frozen atmosphere may turn to gas. The dwarf planet then would look rocky.

Important Discoveries Beyond Pluto

1950
Astronomer Jan Oort suggests that a band of space objects lies at the outer reaches of the solar system. He names it the Oort Cloud.

1951
Astronomer Gerard Kuiper suggests that a band of icy objects exists near to Pluto.

Sedna

Eris is the largest known KBO. But it's not the farthest object from the sun. Sedna is the most distant object discovered thus far. At its farthest point, it is about 82 billion miles (132 billion km) from the sun. That's almost 900 times the distance from the sun to Earth. Sedna is so far away from the sun that it takes 10,500 Earth years to complete one orbit!

1992

Astronomers find a 100-mile-wide object beyond Pluto. Kuiper was correct. The region is named the Kuiper Belt.

2003

Astronomers discover Sedna, a space object that might be in the Oort Cloud. However, Sedna looks like a KBO. There is still no proof that the Oort Cloud exists.

Optics

Inside Hubble are two mirrors, the primary and secondary mirrors.

Primary Mirror
Diameter: 94.5 inches (2.4 m)
Weight: 1,825 pounds (828 kg)

Secondary Mirror
Diameter: 12 inches (0.3 m)
Weight: 27.4 pounds (12.3 kg)

Hubble Facts

Length: 43.5 feet (13.2 m)
Weight: 24,500 pounds (11,110 kg)
Maximum diameter: 14 feet (4.2 m)

The Hubble Space Telescope

Hubble is the world's first space-based optical telescope. Every 97 minutes, Hubble orbits around Earth. It moves at nearly 5 miles (8 km) per second. That means it travels across the United States in about 10 minutes! As it travels, Hubble's mirrors reflect light and send it to scientific instruments. The instruments process the data and then send results to scientists on Earth. Hubble transmits about 120 gigabytes of science data every week. If that amount of information was printed in books, the books would fill a shelf almost 3,600 feet (1,097 m) long.

Energy Source: The Sun

Two 25-foot (8-m) solar panels, or arrays, capture the sun's energy.

27

A comet called NEAT flew near Earth in 2001. Comets are made of ice and rock. When they pass close to the sun, some of their ice turns to gas and dust. Gas and dust form a comet's tail.

Tail

Comet

CHAPTER 4

What Else Is Out There?

 A comet's tail can be more than 6 million miles long!

KBOs are still mysterious to astronomers. However, they do know what happens to some KBOs as they get closer to the sun. KBOs may leave the Kuiper Belt and become comets. Comets are large chunks of rock and ice that travel around the sun.

This image shows fragments of Comet 73P, which orbits the sun about every five and a half years. In 1995, this comet broke into three pieces. It has since crumbled into several dozen pieces.

Comets

Comets orbit the sun in an oval shape. When a comet is headed toward the sun, its head is in front. If a comet gets close to the sun, some ice turns to gas, and dust sprays outward. These gases and dust form the comet's tail. The comet's head points toward the sun, and the tail points away from it.

Most comets take less than 200 years to orbit the sun. Other comets are much farther out in space, so they have larger orbits. The farthest ones take thousands of years to orbit the sun. These distant comets may come from a mysterious area currently known as the **Oort Cloud**.

Comet Hale-Bopp was discovered in July 1995. Gases form a long, blue tail in this photo. Dust forms the yellowish tail.

The Oort Cloud

Nobody is sure whether an area called the Oort Cloud exists. No telescope can see objects that small and dark, that far away. Some astronomers think there are clouds of space objects 18 trillion miles

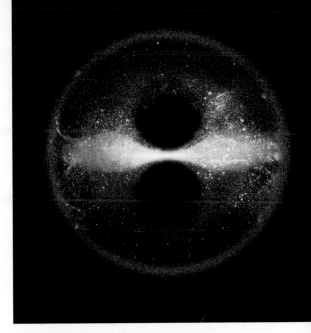

An artist drew this illustration of the Oort Cloud.

(30 trillion km) from the sun. The Oort Cloud may form the outer edge of Earth's solar system. Some astronomers also think there may be more than a trillion comets in the Oort Cloud!

A comet that gets too close to the sun breaks into smaller chunks, dust, and gases.

This is an illustration of the Milky Way galaxy. A galaxy is a huge collection of stars, gases, dust, and other material. The Milky Way could hold as many as a trillion stars! Earth's solar system is part of the Milky Way.

CHAPTER 5

What Are Other Solar Systems Like?

If the galaxy were an 80-mile-long highway, Earth's solar system would equal less than 1 inch of that highway.

The planets and other objects in our solar system orbit the sun. Did you know that the sun is really a star? There are billions of stars just like it. Astronomers have found other solar systems. They are working to learn more about them.

The bright blue spots in this photo are newly-formed stars in a galaxy near to ours. The Hubble Space Telescope took this photo.

33

Planet Search

Since 1995, astronomers have found more than 200 planets orbiting other stars. These planets seem very different from Earth. Some are very close to their stars, so they are boiling hot. Others are very far from their stars and might be very cold. Some seem to be gas giants without solid surfaces.

If there is another planet where life exists, it would probably need liquid water. All forms of life on Earth need water to survive.

This illustration shows planets orbiting a star named Gliese 581 in another solar system.

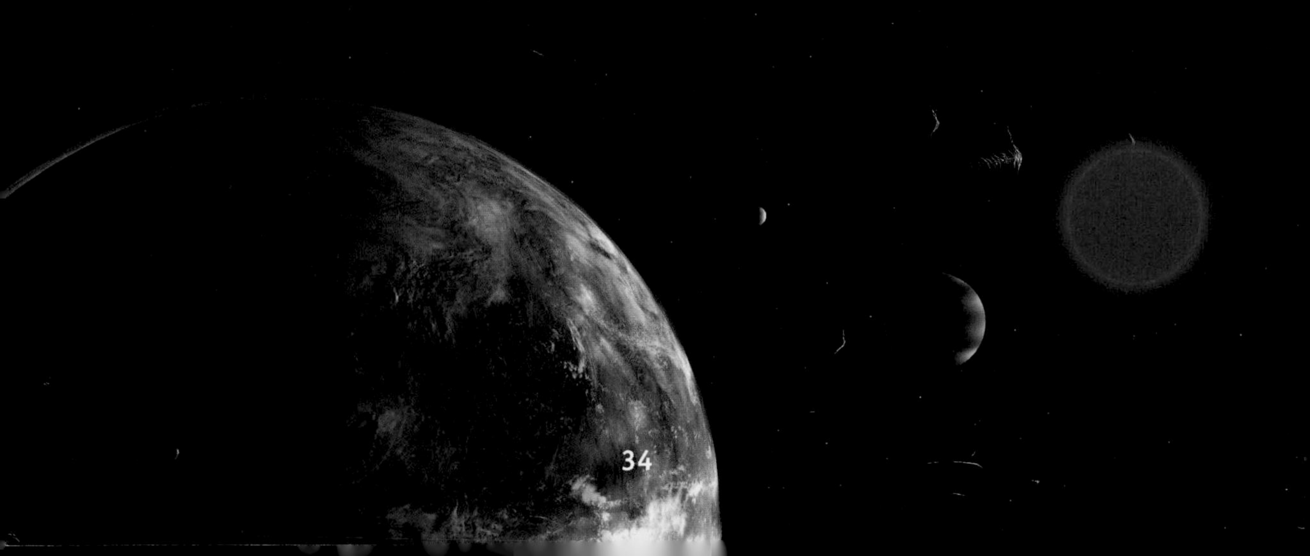

Earth's atmosphere contains a variety of gases that are necessary for life on the planet. The atmosphere is shown in blue in this drawing.

The right atmosphere is also important for life to exist. On Earth, living things use gases in the atmosphere to survive. An atmosphere can also keep a planet from getting too hot or too cold. Earth's atmosphere blocks some of the sun's rays during the day and holds on to some heat at night.

In April 2007, astronomers announced they had found a planet that they thought might be like Earth. They call this planet Gliese (GLEE-zuh) 581 c. Later that year, astronomers discovered that this planet is probably too hot to support life. But another planet, Gliese 581 d, might have the right temperatures for life. Astronomers will need to study the planet more to find out if life exists there.

You would see a giant red sun from Gliese 581 c.

On its way to the edge of our solar system, *Voyager 1* visited Jupiter and Saturn. *Voyager 1* was the first space probe to provide detailed images of the moons of these planets.

CHAPTER 6

Missions Beyond Pluto

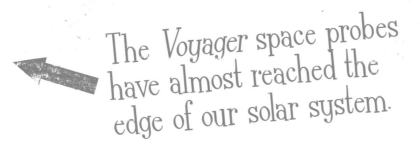

The *Voyager* space probes have almost reached the edge of our solar system.

Astronomers use **space probes** to learn more about what's beyond our solar system. Space probes are spaceships that do not have astronauts on board. A few space probes have almost traveled beyond our solar system. Two of these are called *Voyager 1* and *Voyager 2*.

The Voyager Missions

Voyager 1 and *Voyager 2* were both launched in 1977. The mission's main goal was to explore Jupiter, Saturn, Uranus, and Neptune. But the probes have continued to travel deeper into space.

Voyager 1 is one of the most distant human-made objects in space. It is now 102 times farther from the sun than Earth is. *Voyager 2* is going in a different direction. It is about 82 times as far from the sun as Earth is.

The Voyager probes gather information about distant points in the solar system. They take hundreds of pictures. Astronomers hope *Voyager 1* and *Voyager 2* will keep sending back information until at least 2020.

New Horizons is traveling at a speed of more than 52,000 miles per hour!

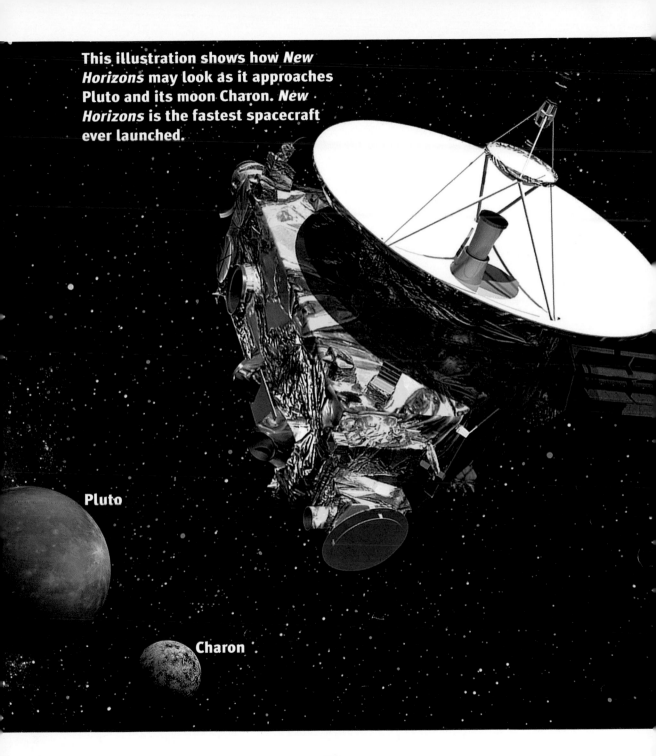

This illustration shows how *New Horizons* may look as it approaches Pluto and its moon Charon. *New Horizons* is the fastest spacecraft ever launched.

Pluto

Charon

New Horizons lifts off from Cape Canaveral on January 19, 2006.

This is an exciting time for space exploration. Tools such as the Hubble Space Telescope have helped astronomers learn more about space. *Voyager 1* and *Voyager 2* are helping astronomers find what is at the outer edge of our solar system. Another space probe, called *New Horizons*, was launched in January 2006. It will fly past Pluto and its moons in 2015. *New Horizons* will then explore the Kuiper Belt until 2020.

Greetings From Earth

Both *Voyager 1* and *Voyager 2* are carrying disks similar to CDs. These disks contain greetings in 55 languages and photographs of Earth and humans.

Beings from another planet will probably never find these disks. But just in case they do, astronomers included instructions on how to play the disks. If other beings played the disks, they would get a glimpse of life on Earth.

The golden disks on *Voyager 1* and *Voyager 2* contain a wide variety of music, including pieces by Beethoven, Chuck Berry, and Navajo Native Americans.

With new instruments and new missions on the way, astronomers think the best is yet to come. Would you like to join them and discover more of what lies beyond Pluto? ★

Campers get to learn about flying a space shuttle at a program called Space Camp.

Minimum distance from the sun to the Kuiper Belt: About 2.8 billion mi. (4.5 billion km)

Number of KBOs identified: More than 1,000

Largest known KBO: Eris

Diameter of Eris: 1,491 mi. (2,400 km)

Second-largest known KBO: Pluto, the former planet

Diameter of Pluto: 1,430 mi. (2,302 km)

Farthest known solar system object: Sedna

Time it takes Sedna to orbit the sun: 10,500 Earth years

Minimum distance from the sun to the Oort Cloud: 18 trillion mi. (30 trillion km)

Did you find the truth?

(T) The Kuiper Belt was discovered by an astronomer who couldn't see it.

(F) No spaceship has ever traveled beyond Pluto.

Resources

Books

Bullock, Linda. *Looking Through a Telescope*. Danbury, CT: Children's Press, 2004.

Carruthers, Margaret W. *The Hubble Space Telescope*. Danbury, CT: Franklin Watts, 2004.

Chrismer, Melanie. *Comets*. Danbury, CT: Children's Press, 2008.

DK Publishing. *Astronomy*. New York: DK Publishing, 2004.

Hansen, Ole Steen. *Space Flight*. New York: Crabtree, 2004.

Kerrod, Robin. *Space Probes*. Milwaukee, WI: World Almanac Library, 2005.

Kortenkamp, Steve. *The Milky Way*. Mankato, MN: Capstone Press, 2008.

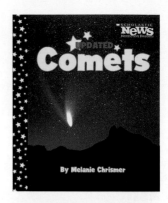

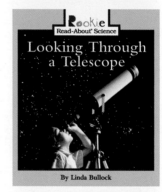

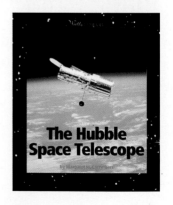

Organizations and Web Sites

National Space Society
1620 I Street NW, Suite 615
Washington, DC 20006
202-429-1600
This organization helps people learn to live and work in space.

Astronomy for Kids—The Universe
www.kidsastronomy.com/deep_space.htm
Check out this site for more on stars, galaxies, and deep space.

SPACE.com: *New Horizons*
www.space.com/missionlaunches/0601_pluto_newhorizons_archive.html
Find out what *New Horizons* is doing right now.

Places to Visit

Kennedy Space Center
Kennedy Space Center, FL 32899
www.ksc.nasa.gov
Take a tour of KSC's giant rockets and launch pads.

Smithsonian National Air and Space Museum
Independence Avenue at 4th Street, SW
Washington, DC 20560
202-633-1000
www.nasm.si.edu
See the world's largest collection of historic airplanes and spaceships.

Important Words

astronomers (uh-STRAW-nuh-murz) – scientists who study the planets, stars, and space

atmosphere (AT-mu-sfihr) – the blanket of gases that surrounds a planet or other object

comets – large chunks of rock and ice that travel around the sun

dwarf planets – bodies in the solar system that orbit the sun, have a constant (nearly round) shape, are not moons, and have orbits that overlap with the orbits of other bodies

gravity – a force that pulls two objects together; gravity pulls you down onto Earth

KBOs – icy, rocky objects that orbit the sun in the distant Kuiper Belt

Kuiper Belt (KY-pur belt) – an area in the outer part of the solar system that contains thousands of small space objects

Oort Cloud – a cloud of comets that may form the outer edge of the solar system—no one is sure that it exists

orbit – to travel around an object such as a sun or planet

solar system (SOH-lur SISS-tuhm) – a sun and all the objects that travel around it

space probes – spaceships that travel without astronauts on board

Index

About the Author

Award-winning author Elaine Landau has a bachelor's degree from New York University and a master's degree in library and information science from Pratt Institute.

She has written more than 300 non-fiction books for children and young adults. Although Ms. Landau often writes on science topics, she especially likes writing about planets and space.

She lives in Miami, Florida, with her husband and son. The trio can often be spotted at the Miami Museum of Science and Space Transit Planetarium. You can visit Elaine Landau at her Web site: www.elainelandau.com.

PHOTOGRAPHS © 2008: Corbis Images: 14 (Bettmann), 32 (Myron Jay Dorf), 42 (Richard T. Nowitz), 6 (Roger Ressmeyer), 4 bottom, 26, 27 (Roger Ressmeyer/NASA), 21 (Ross Pictures), 8 top right (Denis Scott), 35 (Tom Van Sant/Geosphere), 41; ESO: 34; Getty Images: 16 (Michal Cizek), 8 bottom right (William Radcliff); NASA: back cover (G. Bernstein and D. Trilling), 33 (ESA/Hubble Heritage Team), 15, 25 right (R. Hurt/JPL-Caltech), 3, 39 (JHUAP/SwRI), 8 left, 24 middle, 36 (JPL), 29 (JPL-Caltech), 8 center (Erich Karkoschka/ESA), 28 (Kitt Peak National Observatory), cover, 23 (A. Schaller/ESA), 9, 24 left, 24 center, 40; Pat Rasch: 18, 19; Photo Researchers, NY: 17 (Chris Butler), 20, 25 left (Mark Garlick), 5 bottom, 12 (Roger Harris), 30 (Jerry Lodriguss), 31 (Claus Lunau/FOCI/Bonnier Pub.), 4 top, 5 top, 10, 11 (Detlev van Ravenswaay) , 7 (M. I. Walker); Scholastic Library Publishing, Inc.: 44.